To my son Andrey,
passionate mushroom picker,
my son Daniel, passionate mushroom eater,
and my husband, Alex, who is both
—K. A.

## AUTHOR'S NOTE

This book is about my passion for mushrooms,
a passion typical of anyone raised in Russia, as I was,
or in China or much of Europe. American parents take joy in
teaching their children to identify flowers, trees, and birds. It is my
hope that this book will help families discover the special excitement
of hunting and naming mushrooms. The book is an introduction to
the world of mushrooms. It is not a field guide intended for use in
identifying mushrooms. For that information consult the books listed
on page 44 and contact your local mycological society. Common
sense tells us not to eat any wild food without first obtaining
expert identification. Some mushrooms are poisonous.
Never eat a mushroom unless you can
positively identify it.
—K. A.

My thanks to mycologists David Arora, University of Santa Cruz; Robert Shaffer, University of Michigan; and Gary Lincoff, New York Botanical Gardens, for checking the manuscript, and to Jill Ciment and Ian Frazier for their support and criticism. Thank you to my enthusiastic editor, Simone Kaplan, and to the most patient of art directors, Martha Rago. —K. A.

SQUARE
FISH

An imprint of Macmillan Publishing Group, LLC
120 Broadway, New York, NY 10271 • mackids.com

Square Fish and the Square Fish logo are trademarks of Macmillan and are used by
Henry Holt and Company under license from Macmillan.

Our books may be purchased in bulk for promotional, educational, or business use.
Please contact your local bookseller or the Macmillan Corporate and Premium Sales Department at
(800) 221-7945 ext. 5442 or by email at MacmillanSpecialMarkets@macmillan.com.

The Library of Congress has cataloged the hardcover edition as follows:
Library of Congress Cataloging-in-Publication Data
Arnold, Katya. [Book of mushrooms] Katya's book of mushrooms / written by Katya Arnold with Sam Swope; illustrated by
Katya Arnold. p. cm. Includes bibliographical references and index. Summary: An introduction to mushrooms with
tips for identifying different kinds. 1. Mushrooms–Juvenile literature. [1. Mushrooms.] I. Swope, Sam. II. Title.
QK617.A685  1996  589.2'22–dc20  95-52598
ISBN 0-8050-4136-2

Originally published in the United States by Henry Holt and Company
First Square Fish edition, 2023
Book designed by Jessica Rodriguez
Square Fish logo designed by Filomena Tuosto
Printed in China by RR Donnelley Asia Printing Solutions Ltd., Dongguan City, Guangdong Province

ISBN 978-1-250-89356-7 (paperback)
1  3  5  7  9  10  8  6  4  2

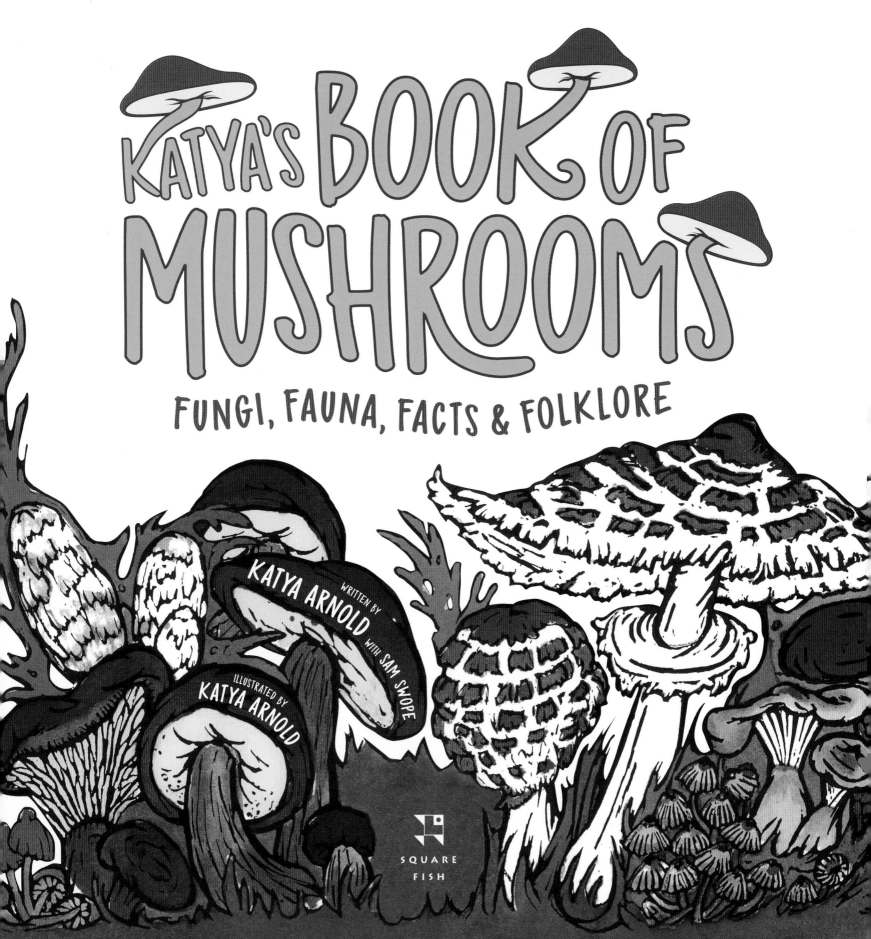

# Katya's BOOK OF MUSHROOMS

## FUNGI, FAUNA, FACTS & FOLKLORE

WRITTEN BY
KATYA ARNOLD
WITH SAM SWOPE

ILLUSTRATED BY
KATYA ARNOLD

SQUARE FISH

HENRY HOLT AND COMPANY · NEW YORK

I am a hunter.

I grew up in Russia. When I was five, I would often go into the woods alone to hunt. I didn't hunt animals or birds. I hunted mushrooms. If I came home with my basket full, everyone praised me, and this made me feel very important. I was feeding my family. I was giving them something substantial, something delicious, something exciting—mushrooms.

I live in a city, but it is in the forest that I feel most at home. There I enter a totally different world. It's green, quiet, with soft light, deep shadows, and an absolutely magnificent smell. I can sense animals hiding behind the trees, and feel the presence of fairies and gnomes. I walk slowly, carefully, looking around. The ground is wet, springy, covered with pine needles. I am hunting mushrooms.

The best time to hunt is in the woods after a rain. I play games with the mushrooms. Sometimes I leave my knife and basket at home and hide a little brown bag in my pocket. I pretend I am just going for a walk and not looking for mushrooms at all. I say, "Oh, I don't care." But when I feel a mushroom is near, I chant gently, "Come to me! Come!"

Mushrooms hide. They trick me. Sometimes they look like leaves. Sometimes I rush toward a mushroom but find it's just a stump. I crawl in the brush, go up and down the hill; I sweat, get very desperate; then I come back to where I began and there the mushrooms are, as if they had been there all along.

Mushrooms have been on the earth for more than forty million years. They are neither plant nor animal—they are fungi. There are more than one hundred thousand varieties of mushrooms. They come in wonderfully strange shapes and colors and pop up suddenly from nowhere in unexpected places, a mysterious gift. Hunting mushrooms is a rare pleasure that doesn't require special equipment, just a curious nature, a love of the outdoors, and sharp eyes.

## What Is a Mushroom?

I love mushrooms for many reasons. Obviously some are tasty to eat. But they are also marvelous to look at, and they come in many different colors. When I pick them out of the moss or dried leaves and needles, I am amazed by how clean and perfectly shaped they are, a true art of nature. They are wonderful to hold. Some are heavy and velvety, like a ripening peach. Others are light, brittle, and shiny like a piece of jewelry. When I turn a mushroom over, I feel the spongy underside or admire the gills, which radiate from the leg like rays from the sun. But whatever the color or shape, mushrooms are all cool and of the earth.

Mushrooms seem like plants, but they don't have chlorophyll, the pigment that makes plants green and helps them produce their own food. Like animals, mushrooms "eat" their food. But they don't have feelings or stomachs, and they don't move around as animals do.

Mushrooms are fungi. Fungi don't reproduce from seeds, like plants, or from eggs, like animals. They reproduce from spores. Most spores are single, simple cells. Every mushroom produces hundreds or even millions of spores, which are carried to different places by the wind and rain, by animals and insects. New fungi grow from the spores. Some spores live for hundreds of years and are so hardy they can survive droughts and freezing cold.

If the conditions are right, a mycelium grows out of the spore. The mycelium is the body of the fungus. It resembles a mass of threads. A mycelium grows underground or beneath tree bark. It takes in food and expels waste. It can be huge, as big as a whole state! Some mycelia live for just a few days and some live for several hundred years. Every now and then, after a rainstorm, they produce new baby (or button) mushrooms.

Mushrooms are the "fruit" of fungi. Their lives can be as short as a couple of hours or as long as many years. Just as a tomato is only part of a much bigger plant, mushrooms are only part of the fungus.

## MUSHROOM *(Agaricus)*
The mushroom is the "fruit" of the fungus

Cap

Gills

Spores

Leg

Button

New mycelium

Mycelium

## PLANT *(Tomato)*
The tomato is the "fruit" of the plant

Leaf

Flower

Sprout

Seeds

Stem

Roots

**HAWK WING, SCALY HEDGEHOG** *(Sarcodon umbricatum)*
This mushroom contains excellent blue or green dyes.

**HEDGEHOG, SWEET TOOTH** *(Hydnum repandum)*

# Mushroom Names

**M**ushrooms often have funny names. When I hunt, I say, "I've got you now, slippery jack!" Or "You are not a prince, you are an old worm-eaten good-for-nothing!" I like to get the whole royal family in my basket, with the king, the queen, the prince, and the commander, but it's also nice to capture a gypsy mushroom or grab a pig's ear, or sneak up on a dead man's finger.

Every country has its own folk names for common mushrooms. There is a mushroom that some Americans call hen-of-the-woods because it looks like a hen roosting under a tree. But in other parts of America it is called sheep's head and, most strangely, cow's mouth. To the Japanese, the same mushroom looks like a dancer's kimono sleeves waving in the air, and there it is called *mai-take*— dancing mushroom. But in every country this mushroom is also known by its scientific name, *Grifola frondosa*, which in Latin means "leafy."

**TURKEY TAIL** *(Trametes versicolor)*
Some people use this fancy mushroom as jewelry.

**WITCH HAT, CONICAL WAXY CAP** *(Hygrocybe conica)*
If you touch this mushroom, it turns from red to black.

**LOBSTER** *(Hypomyces lactifluorum)*

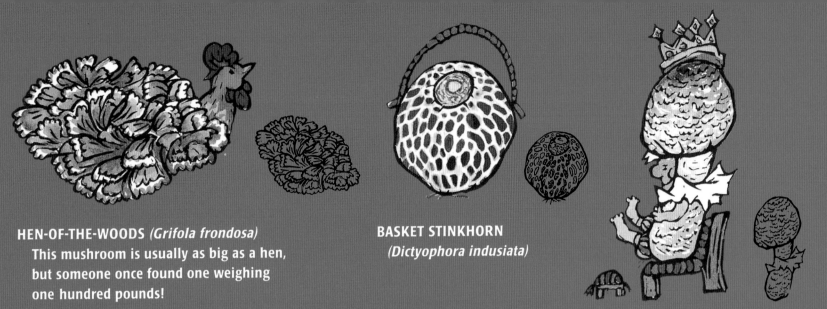

**HEN-OF-THE-WOODS** *(Grifola frondosa)*
This mushroom is usually as big as a hen, but someone once found one weighing one hundred pounds!

**BASKET STINKHORN**
*(Dictyophora indusiata)*

**PRINCE** *(Agaricus augustus)*

Scientific names, which are always Latin or Greek, are the same throughout the world and often offer interesting information about the mushroom. For instance, one little mushroom with a smooth reddish cap is called *Dermocybe californica*. *Dermo* means skin, and *cybe* means head. So it is a skinhead from California! Sometimes a mushroom's scientific name pays tribute to a person, like *Boletus barrowsii*, which honors Chuck Barrows, who pioneered the study of mushrooms in the southwestern United States. Or the scientific name may tell you where the mushroom was discovered, such as *Suillus sibiricus*, which was first found in Siberia. Guidebooks usually refer to mushrooms by their scientific names.

**OLD-MAN-OF-THE-WOODS**
*(Strobilomyces floccopus)*

**OCTOPUS STINKHORN** *(Clathrus archeri)*
This pretty mushroom has a totally disgusting smell.

**SATAN'S BOLETE** *(Boletus satanas)*
This poisonous mushroom has a red underside. If you break it open, it turns blue. Be cautious!

# The Mushroom Feast

Mushrooms are not only delicious, they are nutritious, too. When I come upon a mushroom that looks as if it's been nibbled, it probably has been—by porcupines or hedgehogs. Sometimes I come across many mushroom legs sticking up from the ground like startled soldiers who have lost their heads. The delicious caps have been eaten by greedy squirrels and chipmunks. They got my mushrooms before I did, and it makes me mad!

I'm not fond of slugs, either. Slugs thrive on mushrooms, and sometimes I pick a mushroom and find ten of those slimy creatures on it. But after I've tossed the slugs away, what's left of the mushroom is mine.

The creature I hate most is a tiny worm with a white body and a black head. It is disgusting and treacherous. All day long I hunt, hunt, hunt. Finally I find a beautiful mushroom that looks perfectly healthy and delicious, but later at home when I eagerly cut it open, I discover the worms are already there, eating my dinner.

Truffles are the most expensive mushrooms of all because they are hard to find and have a divine flavor. The French call the BLACK TRUFFLE *(Tuber melanosporum)* the black diamond, and one pound of them costs as much as a good computer. In America truffles grow in Texas, California, and Oregon.

Truffles grow underground, where humans cannot find them. But certain animals are trained to sniff them out, and when they start digging excitedly, then you know that truffles have been found.

Goats lead Italians to truffles and bear cubs find them in Russia.

In France pigs are used, but they must be muzzled or they will quickly gobble up all the truffles they find. Another problem with the pigs is they are so lazy, the farmers must carry them all the way to the forest and back. Because the farmers are lazy too, they now prefer to use dogs, who love to run in the woods sniffing out truffles but don't like to eat them.

# More Mushroom Lovers

**O**nce after a mushroom hunt on an island off the coast of Maine, I sat on the beach to sort my catch. I had found some beautiful aspen boletes, which have round, robust red caps, and these I put at the far end of my towel. Before long a seagull darted down and stole one away. I laughed and thought, "He's mistaken the mushroom for a crab!" Soon he was back for another, and I realized he wasn't mistaking anything—he really liked the mushrooms. But when he came back for a third, I shooed him away and said, "That's all you get for now!"

All over the world mushrooms are eaten by people as well as animals. Pigs, cows, donkeys, deer, moose, reindeer, squirrels, turtles, mice, and kangaroos love mushrooms as much as I do.

The Kaibab squirrel of Arizona is a very picky eater. Captive squirrels reject all other food when mushrooms are available.

In India and Pakistan the OYSTER MUSHROOM *(Pleurotus eryngii)* is dried and fed to donkeys. In America our donkeys eat oats and we eat the mushrooms.

Siberian reindeer are said to be crazy about FLY AGARIC (*Amanita muscaria*). It seems to make them happy and perhaps has some medicinal value.

**BIRD'S-NEST MUSHROOMS**
(Spores on inner surface)

Not all mushrooms have the familiar cap and leg. Some look like coral, some like cups; others resemble balls, or fans, or even brains. Where the spores are found helps us to separate mushrooms into basic groups. Here are some of the major groups of mushrooms.

**GILLED MUSHROOMS**
(Spores on the gills)

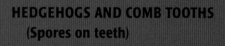

**HEDGEHOGS AND COMB TOOTHS**
(Spores on teeth)

**BOLETES**
(Spores in spongy underside)

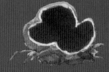

**CUP FUNGI AND MORELS**
(Spores in pits)

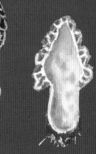

**STINKHORNS**
(Spores ripen inside the egg, then shoot up on a slimy, stinking stem to attract flies)

**TRUFFLES**
(Spores inside)

# Kinds of Mushrooms

**O**nce I went mushroom hunting with a friend, and she found something horrifying. It looked like a piece of cheese with drops of blood on it. I had never seen such a mushroom before, and the guidebook identified it as red-juice tooth (*Hydnellum peckii*).

This is the wonderful thing about mushrooms. Almost every time I go hunting, I find one I've never seen. Mushrooms come in an unbelievable variety of shapes and sizes. Conifer coral mushrooms look like frozen waterfalls made of cream. Morels can be strangely textured, like brown or black honeycombs. Chanterelles are completely different, like bright orange trumpets lighting up the dark forest. Shaggy parasols resemble hats, and mycenas might be tiny umbrellas.

The list goes on and on, and still new mushrooms are being found. There are many things we do not know about mushrooms, so there is a lot of room for new discoveries about them.

**PUFFBALLS AND EARTHSTARS**
(Spores inside)

**CHANTERELLES**
(Spores on the outer surface
of shallow, irregular gills)

**POLYPORES**
(Spores in tiny tubes)

# Learning about Mushrooms

One October my older brother Dima, who is a great mushroom hunter, rode out on his bicycle and came back red faced, with his backpack stuffed with honey mushrooms. I was a little girl, and I watched in amazement as he emptied his backpack. The mushrooms just kept coming and coming and coming, like circus clowns from a car. They took up the whole table. Honey mushrooms are like sponges. You can squish them and they spring back to their original shape.

While we cleaned the mushrooms, Dima made me smell them and touch them. "Pay attention," he said. "See how the legs are long and stringy? See how the caps are hairy and humped?" Then he said, "Do we call them honey mushrooms because bees like them?" "Yes," I guessed. "Dumbbell!" he said. "We call them that because they're the color of honey."

This was the way I learned to identify mushrooms.

Honey mushrooms grow on trees or stumps, like a bouquet of flowers. If you try to pull one from the tree, you get the surrounding ones as well. They are connected by the mycelium in the wood.

he mushrooms I do not know, I consult
oks, comparing the different pictures and
, and I make spore prints. The color of
ints is a reliable help in identification. I
mushroom I am not absolutely sure of.

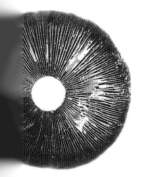

ke a spore print:

1. Find a ripe mushroom, not too young, not too old. Supermarket mushrooms work fine.
2. Cut off the leg.
3. Put the cap on a white piece of paper, gill- or pore-side down.
4. Cover the cap with a drinking glass.
5. Leave it alone, and within two to twenty-four hours you will find a beautiful print on the paper.

# Identifying Mushrooms

**B**ecause some mushrooms are dangerous to eat, hunters must be able to absolutely identify their catch. It is not always easy to identify mushrooms. When I find an unfamiliar mushroom, I bring it home, identify it in three separate guidebooks, consult my mushroom friends, and throw it away. Then I wait until I have found that particular mushroom enough times that I can recognize it without the guide. Then and only then do I eat it.

To identify a mushroom, you must first know the answers to these questions:

| What is its shape? | What's underneath the cap? | Does it have anything on its leg? | What color is its cap? |
| --- | --- | --- | --- |
| Cap and leg<br>Brainlike<br>Cup<br>Coral<br>Ball | Gills<br>Tubes/Sponge<br>Spines | Plain<br>Ring only<br>Sac only<br>Ring and sac<br>Web | Its leg?<br>Its spores?<br>Its flesh?<br>Does its color change when you touch it?<br>How big is it? |

## THINGS TO CHECK:

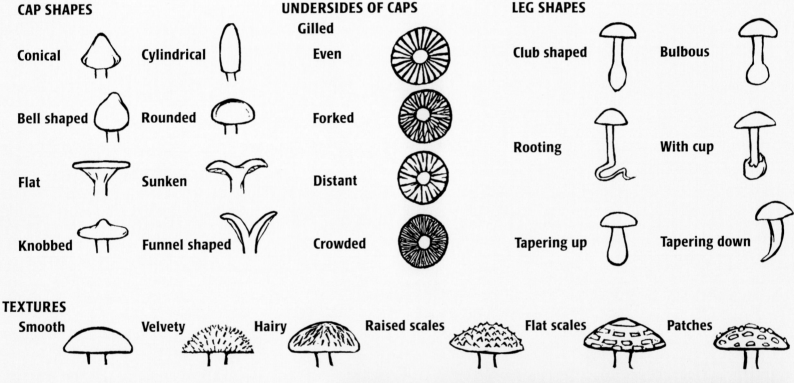

**CAP SHAPES**

Conical    Cylindrical

Bell shaped    Rounded

Flat    Sunken

Knobbed    Funnel shaped

**UNDERSIDES OF CAPS**

Gilled

Even

Forked

Distant

Crowded

**LEG SHAPES**

Club shaped    Bulbous

Rooting    With cup

Tapering up    Tapering down

**TEXTURES**

Smooth    Velvety    Hairy    Raised scales    Flat scales    Patches

You also need to feel its texture. Some mushrooms are hard like wood, others are brittle like crackers, and some feel smooth like cheddar cheese or soft as butter. Consider where and when the mushroom grew, and smell it. Many mushrooms smell like the earth, but some smell like licorice, some like garlic, others like cucumbers, and some like swimming pools.

Like humans, mushrooms change as they grow older. Young ones are fresh looking and firm. Old ones are scarred, tattered, tough, and often soggy. The cap changes shape and color. The leg usually just gets longer.

### WHAT KIND OF MUSHROOM IS THIS?
This mushroom has a cap and a leg.
· The cap is orange and rounded, with raised scales.
· The leg is bulbous, light orange, with a ring and scales.
· Under the cap the gills are pale yellow and even.
· The mushroom is medium sized, about 3 inches high.
· When cut, the flesh is white. It doesn't change color when you touch it.
· It was found under a conifer.
· The smell is pleasant.
It is an *Amanita flavoconia*, also known as yellow patches.

If you keep your eyes open, you'll find mushrooms almost everywhere.

Sometimes on the street where I live, I see an explosion of tiny INKY CAPS *(Coprinus atramentarius)* growing out of the sidewalk. These mushrooms live just two or three hours. They're very fragile and must be eaten soon after picking or they turn into a black liquid.

If your living room has recently been flooded, you might find some DOMESTIC CAP fungus *(Peziza domiciliana)* in your carpet.

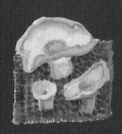

SHAGGY MANES *(Coprinus comatus)* stand side by side like soldiers. Once a thousand were counted in a single field.

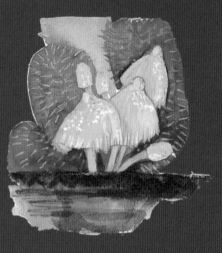

YELLOW PARASOLS *(Lepiota lutea)* are found in flowerpots, a guest of your house plants.

SNOWBANK FALSE MORELS *(Gyromitra gigas)* grow in melting snow in early spring. They are the first mushrooms of the season.

Look for PARASOL MUSHROOMS *(Lepiota procera)* in lawns and pastures.

WALNUT MYCENA *(Mycena luteopallens)* grow—guess where?

DESERT STALK PUFFBALLS *(Battarraea stevensii)* grow in the desert after a rain.

**WHITE MARASMIUS MUSHROOMS**
*(Marasmiellus albuscorticis)*
grow in rows on dead twigs and branches.

**CUITLACOCHE or CORN SMUT MUSHROOMS**
*(Ustilago maydis)* grow out of corn kernels,
making your corn on the cob look disgusting,
but the mushrooms taste delicious
and are very popular in Mexico.

# Where Mushrooms Live

**M**ushrooms grow everywhere, and wherever I am, there they are. When I *expect* to find mushrooms somewhere, however, I never do. Once I went all the way to Siberia because it is famous as a place where mushrooms are found in great abundance, but of course I found nothing. On the other hand, I have also found them where I never thought they could grow, such as in the desert.

In Moscow, where I grew up, there is an enormous museum in the center of the city. One day the sidewalks around the museum began to lift up quite mysteriously. People thought there must have been an earthquake or underground explosion. But when they looked under the sidewalks, they found thousands and thousands of white button mushrooms. Years before, there had been a stable on that spot and the ground was still rich with horse manure. The manure fed these tiny mushrooms that together lifted giant slabs of sidewalk!

So you can see how stubborn and insistent mushrooms are. They can grow almost anywhere—underwater, in snowbanks, in sand, in backyards, baseball fields, city streets, and even in your carpet after a flood. According to mushroom author David Arora, some mysterious coprinus mushrooms once invaded the floor of his car!

**POWDER CAPS** *(Asterophora lycoperdoides)* grow on other mushrooms.

The tiny **ORANGE PINWHEEL MARASMIUS** mushrooms *(Marasmius siccus)* grow on leaves.

**SWAMP BEACONS** *(Mitrula paludosa)* grow in wet soil, bogs, and temporary pools in woods.

# Mushroom Hunting

The best place to hunt mushrooms is a forest, but finding them there isn't always easy. It's important not to be lazy and to examine everything, because mushrooms can look like leaves or bark or flowers. To be a successful hunter, it helps to know where and when mushrooms grow. Often you find mushrooms among tree roots. The side of a forest road might reward you. Shady riverbanks and lakeshores are a good bet. Be sure, too, to look under fir trees and in any mossy areas. And remember, many mushrooms return to the same spots year after year. Once you find your first mushroom, an amazing thing happens. Others follow.

Where I live, the best time to go mushroom hunting is the fall. That's true for most of Europe, too. That is when I find the greatest variety, because most mushrooms like the rain and cooler weather. But I wouldn't look for morels in the fall because they grow only in the spring. In the summer I watch for chanterelles and slippery jacks.

When I find a mushroom, I first try to identify it. Then I might just touch it gently and leave it be. Or I might keep it to use as a decoration. But usually I will put it in my basket and bring it home to eat. I think of mushrooms as food. Some I dry for winter soups, some I pickle, and some I cook for a feast the very same day I find them. Those mushrooms that I do not recognize I bring home in a separate bag to identify.

The quickest and easiest way to learn how to hunt mushrooms is to go to the woods with experienced mushroom hunters. They'll show mushrooms to you and name them; they'll tell you when's the best time to go mushroom hunting in your area. They might share recipes and maybe even bring you home for a mushroom dinner. But don't expect them to tell you their favorite mushroom patches! To find these people, phone your local mycological society.

When I go mushrooming, I wear old sneakers, a long-sleeved shirt, and long pants to protect me from ticks and brambles, I take a knife and my basket and a couple of brown bags so I can separate unknown and possibly poisonous mushrooms from the others. (Never put mushrooms in plastic; they need to breathe.) And I always take along an apple and a sandwich in case I get hungry, because you can't eat wild mushrooms raw.

# Poisonous Mushrooms

**W**hen I was first learning about mushrooms, my brother Dima made sure I was scared to death of the poisonous ones. He told me if I even touched a destroying angel and then put my finger in my mouth, I would drop dead on the spot. Of course this was completely untrue. You can handle any mushroom, even a poisonous one, but if you lick, bite, or eat a poisonous mushroom, it can make you sick.

Never, never, never eat a mushroom you do not recognize. Poisonous mushrooms are powerful. They can kill you. There are just a few truly poisonous mushrooms, so learn to identify these first. When you know to avoid them, you will feel proud and safe.

People who think they may have eaten a poisonous mushroom should immediately contact their poison control center. If you can, save a sample of the suspicious mushroom for identification. Here are two to watch out for.

**CLEFT-FOOT AMANITA** *(Amanita brunnescens)*
Like most amanitas, this mushroom has a bulbous leg and should be avoided. The bulb has distinct cracks, and its brown cap has white patches.

**JACK-o'-LANTERN** *(Omphalotus olearius)*
The poisonous jack-o'-lantern grows in clusters on dead wood and glows in the dark. It is yellowish orange inside and out, and its gills are deep and thin. Jack-o'-lanterns are sometimes carelessly mistaken for chanterelles, but it's easy to tell the difference. Unlike jack-o'-lanterns, chanterelles are white inside, have shallow gills, grow on the ground, and are never found in clusters.

Beware of the LBMs! LBM stands for Little Brown Mushroom. These mushrooms are quite common and some of them are very dangerous.

**DEADLY GALERINA** *(Galerina autumnalis)*
This LBM has a sticky bald cap and grows on dead wood. Its spores are brown, and it has a ring or the trace of a ring on its leg. You never find it in large clusters. The Deadly Galerina is deadly poisonous, but so small it's hard to find, and therefore seldom eaten.

**POISON PIE** *(Hebeloma crustuliniforme)*
A little larger and more attractive than most LBMs, this mushroom has a sticky cap that's the color of a pie crust. Its gills are pale and its stalk is flaky. It smells like a radish and can really upset your stomach.

**FIBER HEAD** *(Inocybe fatigiata)*
The cap of this LBM is dry and scaly with split edges. It has an unpleasant smell. The Fiber Head is not deadly, but it will make you pretty sick.

Every part of the destroying angel is deadly, even the spores.

**DESTROYING ANGEL, CROSS SECTION**

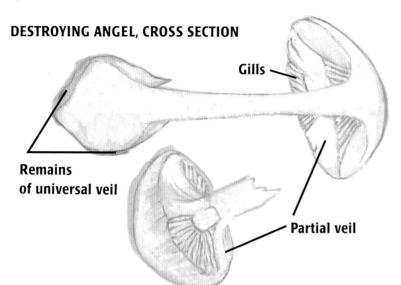

Gills

Remains of universal veil

Partial veil

Of all the thousands of mushrooms in the world, only a small proportion are poisonous. Most of these will only upset your stomach. Very few mushrooms are deadly. But those that are can kill you. Because of the achievements of modern medicine, only about 5 percent of people who eat deadly mushrooms don't survive. But . . . *never* take a risk. Never eat any wild mushroom you cannot identify. WHEN IN DOUBT, THROW IT OUT!

# The Destroying Angel

**S**ome poisonous mushrooms are not very distinctive looking. The destroying angel is. Other mushrooms may look misshapen or dirty or infested, but never this one. It is always absolutely beautiful, slender, shiny, and intensely white. It stands there in the dark woods, gleaming, a vicious queen of death who calls to you, "Come pick me! Eat me!" And you know that this beauty has death in it.

The destroying angel is said to be delicious, and after eating it people live for some time without feeling the least effect. Then, quite suddenly, they get violently ill and some eventually die. But the destroying angel is easy to identify, and there is no need to be afraid of it if you're watchful.

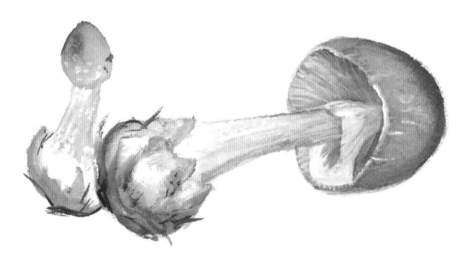

The destroying angel has a homely and poisonous sister called the death cap *(Amanita phalloides)*, which has a greenish or yellow tint, but both have a ring at the top of the leg and the same sac around the base of the leg.

**Beware of them both!**

The deadly destroying angel looks like the delicious meadow mushroom. Take a stick and dig the mushroom out of the ground. If you see a sac at the bottom of the leg, hanging like a loose, floppy bag, you will know this mushroom is really the destroying angel, the most poisonous mushroom known to man.

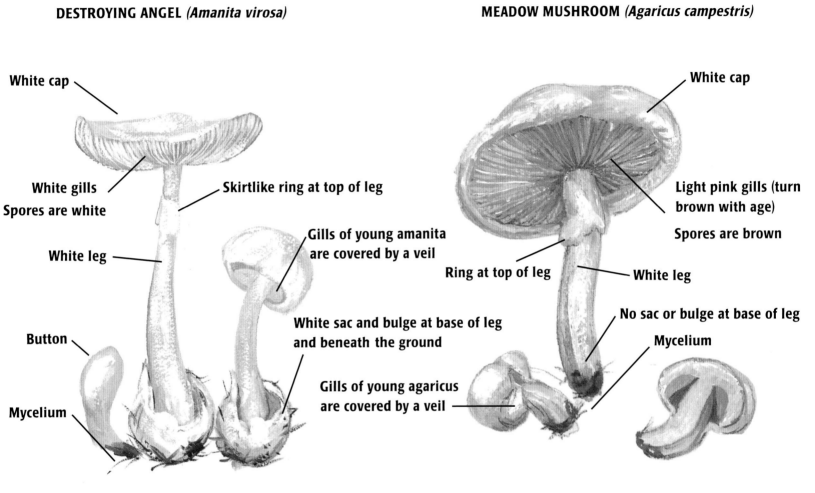

**DESTROYING ANGEL** *(Amanita virosa)*

**MEADOW MUSHROOM** *(Agaricus campestris)*

White cap

White gills
Spores are white

Skirtlike ring at top of leg

White leg

Gills of young amanita are covered by a veil

Button

White sac and bulge at base of leg and beneath the ground

Mycelium

Gills of young agaricus are covered by a veil

White cap

Light pink gills (turn brown with age)

Spores are brown

Ring at top of leg

White leg

No sac or bulge at base of leg

Mycelium

The destroying angel's button looks like that of a young puffball, but you can tell the difference by slicing it from top to bottom. If the inside is solid white, you've found a puffball. But if you see the outline of a cap and leg, like a ghost of the mushroom to come, you'll know you've met a deadly enemy.

**DESTROYING ANGEL, BUTTON STAGE, CROSS SECTION**

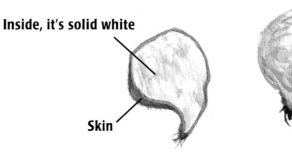

Sac

Outline of cap and leg

**PUFFBALL, CROSS SECTION**

Inside, it's solid white

Skin

# Fly Agaric

Fly agaric is a cheerful-looking poisonous mushroom. It won't kill you, but it will make you very sick. It's extremely pretty—bright red or yellow or orange with little white dots. Fly agaric rarely hides in the darkness of the woods. It likes to be seen.

Fly agaric is also known as the toadstool. According to legend, this mushroom gives its white warts to any toads who sit on it, and the toads pass the warts on to people. Some people sprinkle fly agaric with sugar water or soak it in milk and then use the liquid to trap flies. Moose are crazy about these mushrooms and eat them without ill effect. Mexicans, Siberian shamans, and Native Americans use fly agaric in religious rituals and as medicine for the sick. The Russian witch Baba Yaga uses this mushroom for evil potions and as medicine.

(Amanita muscaria) comes in different
ypically has white dots, which are
the veil that covered the young
This mushroom can grow bigger than
te.

Mushrooms are often found in folklore. Ge
legend has it that long ago the devil quarr
an old witch. He cut her into thousands of
scattered them in the woods. Wherever a p
morel grew, and that is why this delicious
mushroom looks like a little old wrinkled
I think she must have been a very good so
considering how tasty morels are.

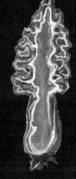

**BLACK MOREL**
*(Morchella elata)*

Sometimes in a healthy lawn you will fin
mushrooms inside of which the grass is p
outside. These circles were once called fa
because it was said that the grass was da
fairies who danced there during the nigh
fairies were unfairly blamed. Now we kn
mushrooms' mycelium that causes the gr
back.

Fly agaric has been known to form rings
hundred mushrooms. What a beautiful si

**FAIRY RING MUSHROOM**
*(Marasmius oreades)*

# Puffballs

**P**uffballs grow in many places: on the roadside, in sports fields, golf courses, and meadows. Once in a city park I saw a round, white plastic shopping bag and became annoyed with people who litter. But when I went over to pick it up, I saw that it wasn't a shopping bag at all. It was a mushroom, a puffball! Puffballs are round. They can be as small as a marble or as large as two feet or more across and weigh up to seventy pounds! When I see an old puffball that has gotten brown and dry, I stomp on it with all my might and a great brown cloud of spores comes out. That's why the Latin name for puffball is *Lycoperdon*, which means wolf fart!

**PUFFBALL**
    Spore case
    Mycelium

Spores

When puffballs get old, the dry skin breaks and the spores are released.

Crows and starlings love to feast on young puffballs.

Some Native American tribes used puffballs for food, medicine, and sacred necklaces and in a game in which players batted the ball back and forth with their hands, trying not to let it hit the ground.

There are more than one hundred types of puffballs in America.

**GEMMED PUFFBALLS** *(Lycoperdon perlatum)*

**PEAR-SHAPED PUFFBALLS** *(Lycoperdon pyriforme)*

**SCULPTURED PUFFBALLS** *(Calbovista sculpta)*

**PASTURE PUFFBALLS** *(Vascellum depressum)*

**PIGSKIN POISON PUFFBALLS** *(Scleroderma citrinum)*

Puffballs often confuse golfers because from a distance they look like golf balls.

Giant puffballs measure from three to twenty-four inches across, can weigh seventy pounds, and may produce 7,000,000,000,000 (7 trillion) spores! If all of these spores were put in a row, they'd circle the earth, and if each spore produced a puffball, which would never happen, the new puffballs would stretch all the way to the sun and back.

**BAROMETER EARTHSTAR** *(Astraeus hygrometricus)* is a close relative of the puffball. It unfolds in wet weather and closes in dry weather.

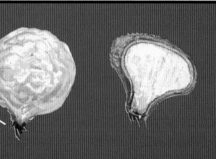

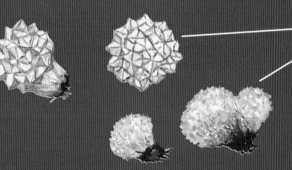

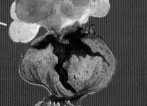

# Chanterelles

One summer I took my basket and my family to the Berkshires. I had heard chanterelles were growing there, but after hours of looking, we hadn't found any. Then I saw them! Well hidden under the low skirt of a fir tree was a brilliant carpet of orange chanterelles growing out of the dead needles. I am always happy when I spot a chanterelle because they grow in groups: when you've found one, you've found dinner. After we had crawled around under the trees for several hours our baskets were full, our pockets were full, and the trunk of our car was full of mushrooms. Sautéed and stored in oil, these mushrooms can last a whole year. We ate ours on New Year's Eve. They had a strong taste and a marvelous smell like the forest they came from.

I now know that chanterelles often grow under conifers or oaks because they need nutrients that are provided by the roots of these trees. In return the mycelia of the chanterelles provide nourishment that makes the trees stronger. They feed each other. Other mushrooms have special partnerships with different trees. Slippery jacks, for example, live only under pine trees; you'll find Satan's boletes only under oaks; and sandy mushrooms are found only at the foot of poplar trees.

**SCALY CHANTERELLE** *(Gomphus floccosus)*

**SMALL CHANTERELLE**
*(Cantharellus minor)*

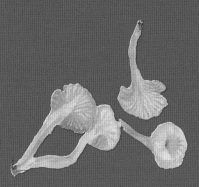

**RED CHANTERELLE** *(Cantharellus cinnabarinus)*

**BLACK TRUMPET** *(Craterellus fallax)*

**CHANTERELLE**
*(Cantharellus cibarius)*

**WHITE CHANTERELLE**
*(Cantharellus subalbidus)*

**BLUE CHANTERELLE**
*(Polyozellus multiplex)*

Chanterelles are a favorite mushroom all over the world. They are marvelous mushrooms, fragrant and tasty and clean and so pretty it almost seems a shame to eat them. In Russia they are called *lisichca*, the little fox. The French call them *crête-de-coq*, the rooster's comb. To the Spanish, they're *cabrito*, the baby goat. For the Poles they're *pieprznik*, the pepper mushroom. And the Japanese call chanterelles *shiba-take*, which means "yellow mushroom that is good to eat." Chanterelle in Latin means "little drinking cup."

Chanterelles come in white, yellow, blue, black, brown, and orange, and they may be large or small, but they are always shaped like a trumpet.

There are more than thirty known different groups of boletes. The undersides of their caps are always spongy and porous. They are only found wild and cannot be cultivated. Many boletes are good to eat, but watch out for those that have red or orange sponge underneath the cap, for they are mildly poisonous.

**TWO-COLORED BOLETE** *(Boletus bicolor)*

**YELLOW FOOT** *(Tylopilus chromapes)*
This gentle bolete has a pinkish cap and a leg that ends in a light-yellow tip.

**BITTER BOLETE** *(Tylopilus felleus)* If you lick this mushroom, you have to spit ten times to get rid of the bitter taste.

**ASPEN BOLETE** *(Leccinum insigne)*
The large size and magnificent colors of this beautiful bolete announce it from far away.

**BIRCH BOLETE**
*(Leccinum scabrum)*

**GOLDSTALK**
*(Boletus ornatipes)*

**LILAC-BROWN BOLETE**
*(Tylopilus eximius)*

**CHESTNUT BOLETE**
*(Gyroporus castaneus)*

**CANDY-APPLE BOLETE**
*(Boletus frostii)*

**SPOTTED BOLETE**
*(Boletus affinis var. maculatus)*

**RHUBARB-STALKED**
**(KING) BOLETE** *(Boletus separans)*

**PAINTED SUILLUS**
*(Suillus pictus)*

**OLD-MAN-OF-THE-WOODS** *(Strobilomyces floccopus)*

## Boletes

**M**any boletes live in a vital relationship with trees. When I go deep into a birch forest, where the white bark shines with a beautiful light, then I know I am likely to find birch boletes. And when I come across an aspen tree large enough to be called a true veteran of this earth, I know if I look hard, eventually I will find a substantial, robust, and handsome mushroom with a firm red head like a potato, the aspen bolete.

# The King Bolete

The king bolete, which grows beneath pine, fir, and oak trees, is the lion of mushrooms—robust, strong, and handsome. It is so delicious you can't eat enough and so special you need a magic chant to help you find one. When I do find one, I scream with delight, startling the forest.

Usually I prefer my mushrooms to be small and young, but with this bolete, bigger is better. When I was little, I'd sometimes find one the size of my head—that was *really* something. I'd put my nose in its velvety cup and breathe its earthy smell, and then I'd carry my treasure carefully with both hands so I wouldn't drop it. At home my family would say, "Ahhh, I never saw a king that big before!" This was always a very proud moment. But then someone else would come along and say, "Oh, I remember Masha found one bigger than that five years ago!" It was our version of a fish story.

**KING BOLETE** *(Boletus edulis)*

Cap

CROSS SECTION

Spongy, porous underside
(made up of tubes)

Leg

Most boletes are mycorrhizal mushrooms, which means they live in a symbiotic or mutually beneficial relationship with a particular tree. The word comes from *myco*, fungus, and *rhiza*, root. Mycorrhizal mushrooms exchange nutrition with trees that grow nearby. The mushrooms can't grow without the trees, and the trees are much healthier when they have mushrooms around. That is one reason mushrooms are so important to the health of our planet.

The largest king bolete ever recorded weighed about thirteen pounds: its cap measured eighteen inches, its leg had a ten-inch diameter, and the mushroom was almost sixteen inches high.

# Polypores

Most polypores grow on trees. Often they stick out from the trunk like shelves, sometimes very fancy shelves. The biggest one, the noble polypore, grows in the western United States and can weigh as much as two adults! Polypore means "many pores," and if you look on the underside of these mushrooms, you will see many tiny holes in which the spores are stored.

I love polypores because even when the woods are bare of other mushrooms, there are polypores. Once I went hunting with Dima in November. The woods were gloomy gray with no bright colors. Then far away we saw the bright orange yellow of a chicken-of-the-woods. This amazing mushroom looks like a huge exotic flower and tastes delicious, a little like chicken. It was so big it took up a whole shelf in the refrigerator and fed us for a week. Of course if was safe to pick because no polypore is ever poisonous if cooked.

Polypores keep the forest clean by helping to break down dead organisms into a rich soil. Without polypores dead grass would choke the meadows and fallen trees, branches, and leaves would litter the forest floor.

**CROWDED PARCHMENT**
*(Stereum complicatum)*

**RED-BELTED POLYPORE**
*(Fomitopsis pinicola)*

**ARTIST'S CONK** *(Ganoderma applanatum)*
You can draw on the white underside of this hard, woody polypore with a stick. A beautiful black line develops in a second.

Although most polypores are tough and woody, some are tender enough to eat.

**CINNABAR-RED POLYPORE**
*(Pycnoporus cinnabarinus)*

**LING CHIH** *(Ganoderma lucidum)*
In Chinese medicine this shiny polypore is called the "marvelous herb of immortality," and some people believe it will even bring a dying person back to life.

**BERKELEY'S POLYPORE**
*(Bondarzewia Berkeleyi)*

**SHINY CINNAMON POLYPORE**
*(Coltricia cinnamomea)*

**WARTED OAK POLYPORE**
*(Inonotus dryadeus)*

**SPLIT GILL**
*(Schizophyllum commune)*

**TRUE TINDER POLYPORE** *(Fomes fomentarius)*
When soaked in urine, salt, and ashes and then dried, this mushroom makes a very good fuse for rifles and excellent kindling. When stewed in hot water, beaten with a mallet, and rubbed, tinder polypore can be used to make clothing, hats, and picture frames.

**QUININE CONK** *(Fomitopsis officinalis)*
These polypores can grow high up in trees, and some mushroom hunters use rifles to shoot them down. They are used as medicine.

**SPRING POLYPORE** *(Polyporus arcularius)*

**BIRCH CONK** *(Piptoporus betutinus)*

**CHICKEN-OF-THE-WOODS**
*(Laetiporus sulphureus)*

**UMBRELLA POLYPORE**
*(Polyporus umbellatus)*

**VIOLET TOOTHED POLYPORE**
*(Trichaptum biformis)*

# Growing Mushrooms at Home

I became very miserable one winter. I was missing mushrooms. I couldn't go out to hunt, and I don't care very much for the mushrooms you find in the supermarket. Then one day I noticed some yellow mold in a flowerpot. When I finally got around to cleaning it out several days later, I was stunned to find a colony of yellow parasols, little lemon yellow mushrooms with amusing conical hats. I was so glad I had not destroyed them!

This gave me the idea to grow my own mushrooms at home. I knew I couldn't grow my favorite bolete in my living room unless I first grew a tree, so I ordered a shiitake mushroom kit. The instructions were easy. First I soaked a small "log" in my biggest pot. Then I put it on a lasagna tray, covered it with a plastic bag, and waited. By the end of the week I saw strange brown bumps on the log. Everybody laughed at me and said no mushrooms would grow. But three days later I triumphantly presented my family with beautifully grown shiitake mushrooms. They were especially tasty, partly because they were so fresh and partly because I grew them myself.

Although you cannot cultivate mycorrhizal mushrooms, such as chanterelles, king boletes, and black trumpets, mushroom pickers go into the woods and collect them for sale in grocery stores. You can hunt them there too. They're always delicious!

The Chinese began cultivating mushrooms two thousand years ago.

In France documents dating to the seventeenth century were found with instructions for growing meadow mushrooms that the French call *champignons (Agaricus campestris)*.

Here in America farmers grow white button *(Agaricus bisporus)*, portobello (also *Agaricus bisporos*), oyster *(Pleurotus ostreatus)*, and shiitake *(Lentinula edodes)* mushrooms indoors year round.

People aren't the only ones to grow mushrooms. Some termites grow them too. Texas leaf-cutting ants *(Atta texana)* cultivate mushrooms in underground nests, cutting leaves in order to feed the mushrooms and ventilating their crop by opening and closing tunnels when needed. They eat only mycelia, however, so people can have the rest!

# GLOSSARY

**Agaric**—a mushroom with gills

**Bolete**—a fleshy mushroom with a sponge underneath its cap

**Button**—a young mushroom before it opens up

**Cap**—the head of a mushroom

**Chlorophyll**—(KLOR-uh-fill)—the substance in plants that makes them green, absorbs sunlight, and helps plants make their own food

**Cluster**—a group of mushrooms attached at the base

**Fairy Ring**—an arc or a circle of mushrooms

**Flesh**—the meaty portion of a mushroom

**Fungus;** Plural, Fungi (FUN-guy)—an organism without chlorophyll that reproduces by spores, such as mushrooms, molds, mildews, and yeasts

**Gills**—the radiating blades on the underside of a mushroom cap

**Leg**—the stemlike part of a mushroom

**Mushroom**—the fruiting body of fungi

**Mycelium** (my-SEEL-ee-um); Plural Mycelia—the rootlike part of fungi; resembles tangled threads

**Mycology**—the scientific study of fungi

**Mycorrhizal Mushroom**—fungus living in partnership with plant roots; each contributes nutrition beneficial to the other

**Parasitic Mushroom**—a mushroom that lives on and feeds off a living animal or plant

**Pores**—tiny holes or openings in boletes and polypores

**Ring**—circular skirt on a mushroom stalk formed by a broken veil

**Sac**—the sacklike cup or tissue surrounding the base of the leg, left after the veil has broken (also known as a volva)

**Sapro/Saprophytic Mushroom**—a mushroom that feeds off dead trees, dung, leaves, litter, or other dead organic matter

**Scales**—raised pieces of broken skin on cap or stalk surface

**Spore**—simple one-cell reproductive unit of a mushroom

**Spore Print**—picture formed on paper by mushroom spores; the print's color and pattern help in identification

**Toadstool**—popular name for a poisonous mushroom

**Tubes**—hollow cylinders containing spores and forming the spongy underside of bolete and polypore caps

**Universal veil**—the tissue that covers and protects a developing mushroom and that breaks as the mushroom grows

## Recommended Books

*All That the Rain Promises and More.* By David Arora. Ten Speed Press, 1991. The book is funny, simple, entertaining, and romantic. It's got lots of basic and clear information. To order, contact Ten Speed Press, P.O. Box 7123, Berkeley, California 94707.

*The Audubon Society Field Guide to North American Mushrooms.* By Gary H. Lincoff. Knopf, 1981. A clear, comprehensive guide with beautiful photographs.

*Mushrooms Demystified.* By David Arora. Ten Speed Press, 1979. A complete and brilliant book. My favorite. Found in any good bookstore.

*Peterson Field Guides: Mushrooms.* By Kent H. McKnight and Vera B. McKnight. Houghton Mifflin, 1987. Easy to use for beginners and found in any good bookstore.

Several mushroom fairs, contests, and festivals are held each year in the United States. For information about them and for the address of the mycological club nearest you, contact the North American Mycological Association, 3556 Oakwood, Ann Arbor, MI 48104-5213, tel. (313) 971-2552, Internet: kwcee@umich.edu

Mushroom-growing kits are available from different plant nurseries and from special mushroom stores.

# INDEX